1/12

Biodiversity

of Temperate Forests

GREG PYERS

Marshall Cavendish
Benchmark

New York

This edition first published in 2012 in the United States of America by
MARSHALL CAVENDISH BENCHMARK
An imprint of Marshall Cavendish Corporation

Website: www.marshallcavendish.us

This publication represents the opinions and views of the author based on Greg Pyer's personal experience, knowledge, and research. The information in this book serves as a general guide only. The author and publisher have used their best efforts in preparing this book and disclaim liability rising directly and indirectly from the use and application of this book.

Other Marshall Cavendish Offices:
Marshall Cavendish International (Asia) Private Limited, 1 New Industrial Road, Singapore 536196 • Marshall Cavendish International (Thailand) Co Ltd. 253 Asoke, 12th Flr, Sukhumvit 21 Road, Klongtoey Nua, Wattana, Bangkok 10110, Thailand • Marshall Cavendish (Malaysia) Sdn Bhd, Times Subang, Lot 46, Subang Hi-Tech Industrial Park, Batu Tiga, 40000 Shah Alam, Selangor Darul Ehsan, Malaysia

Marshall Cavendish is a trademark of Times Publishing Limited

All websites were available and accurate when this book was sent to press.

Library of Congress Cataloging-in-Publication Data

Pyers, Greg.
    Biodiversity of temperate forests / Greg Pyers.
       p. cm. — (Biodiversity)
    Includes index.
    Summary: "Discusses the variety of living things in the ecosystem of a temperate forest"—Provided by publisher.
    ISBN 978-1-60870-532-0
    1. Forest biodiversity—Juvenile literature. 2. Forest ecology—Juvenile literature.
    3. Endangered ecosystems—Juvenile literature. I. Title.
    QH86.P943 2012
    577.3—dc22

                                    2010037464

First published in 2011 by
MACMILLAN EDUCATION AUSTRALIA PTY LTD
15–19 Claremont Street, South Yarra 3141

Visit our website at www.macmillan.com.au or go directly to www.macmillanlibrary.com.au

Associated companies and representatives throughout the world.

Publisher: Carmel Heron
Commissioning Editor: Niki Horin
Managing Editor: Vanessa Lanaway
Editor: Georgina Garner
Proofreader: Tim Clarke
Designer: Kerri Wilson
Page layout: Raul Diche
Photo researcher: Wendy Duncan (management: Debbie Gallagher)
Illustrator: Richard Morden (illustration on p. 10 by Alan Laver, Shelly Communications)
Production Controller: Vanessa Johnson

Printed in China

Acknowledgments
The author and publisher are grateful to the following for permission to reproduce copyright material:

Front cover photograph: Two male deer in Park Dyrehaven, Denmark courtesy of photolibrary/Pierre Vernay.
Back cover photographs courtesy of istockphoto/Vladimir Chernyanskiy (wisent); Le Do (leaves).

Photographs courtesy of:
ANTphoto.com.au/Mrs JM Soper, **15**; Corbis/Yann Arthus-Bertrand, **17**, /Raymond Gehman, **27**, **29**; photolibrary/age fotostock/John Cancalosi, **25**, /Alamy/Jason Edwards, **21**, /Alamy/David Noton, **14**, /Britain on View/Nature Picture Library, **7**, /Gary Lewis, **4**, /SPL/Bob Gibbons, **9**; Shutterstock/Aleksander Bolbot, **28**, /Sandra Caldwell, **18**, /Steffen Foerster Photography, **22**, /Jeffrey M Frank, **20**, /Hydromet, **11**, /Henrik Larsson, **23**, /Peter Weber, **13**. Background and design images used throughout courtesy of Shutterstock/Borislav Gnjidic, (beech forest), / Chukov (autumn trees).

Other material: Maps, US Forestry Service/William B Greeley, **16**.

Please note
At the time of printing, the Internet addresses appearing in this book were correct. Owing to the dynamic nature of the Internet, however, we cannot guarantee that all these addresses will remain correct.

1 3 5 6 4 2

Contents

Glossary Words

When a word is printed in **bold**, you can look up its meaning in the Glossary on page 31.

What Is Biodiversity?

Biodiversity, or biological diversity, describes the variety of living things in a particular place, in a particular **ecosystem**, or across the entire Earth.

Measuring Biodiversity

The biodiversity of a particular area is measured on three levels:

- **species** diversity, which is the number and variety of species in the area.
- genetic diversity, which is the variety of **genes** each species has. Genes determine the characteristics of different living things. A variety of genes within a species enables it to **adapt** to changes in its environment.
- ecosystem diversity, which is the variety of **habitats** in the area. A diverse ecosystem has many habitats within it.

Species Diversity

Some habitats, such as coral reefs and rain forests, have very high biodiversity. In one study of a rain forest in Peru, 283 tree species were found growing in just 2.5 acres (0.01 square kilometers). In the whole of the United States and Canada, there are just 700 tree species.

Habitats and Ecosystems

Temperate forests are habitats, which are places where plants and animals live. Within a forest habitat, there are many smaller habitats, sometimes called microhabitats. Some forest habitats are the forest floor, the tree trunks, and the treetops. Different kinds of **organisms** live in these places. The animals, plants, other living things, nonliving things, and all the ways they affect each other make up a forest ecosystem.

Koalas and eucalyptus trees are part of the biodiversity of an Australian temperate forest.

Biodiversity Under Threat

The variety of species on Earth is under threat. There are somewhere between 5 million and 30 million species on Earth. Most of these species are very small and hard to find, so only about 1.75 million of these species have been described and named. These are called known species.

Scientists estimate that as many as fifty species become **extinct** every day. Extinction is a natural process, but human activities have sped up the rate of extinction by up to one thousand times.

Known Species of Organisms on Earth

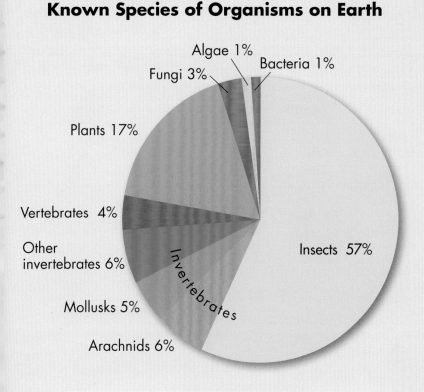

- Algae 1%
- Bacteria 1%
- Fungi 3%
- Plants 17%
- Vertebrates 4%
- Other invertebrates 6%
- Mollusks 5%
- Arachnids 6%
- Insects 57%
- Invertebrates

The known species of organisms on Earth can be divided into bacteria, algae, fungi, plant, and animal species. Animal species are further divided into vertebrates and invertebrates.

Approximate Numbers of Known Vertebrate Species

ANIMAL GROUP	KNOWN SPECIES
Fish	31,000
Birds	10,000
Reptiles	8,800
Amphibians	6,500
Mammals	5,500

Why Is Biodiversity Important?

Biodiversity is important for many reasons. The diverse organisms in an ecosystem take part in natural processes essential to the survival of all living things. Biodiversity produces food and medicine. It is also important to people's quality of life.

Natural Processes

Humans are part of many ecosystems. Our survival depends on the natural processes that go on in these ecosystems. Through natural processes, air and water are cleaned, waste is decomposed, **nutrients** are recycled, and disease is kept under control. Natural processes depend on the organisms that live in the soil, on the plants that produce oxygen and absorb **carbon dioxide**, and on the organisms that break down dead plants and animals. When species of organisms become extinct, these natural processes may stop working.

Food

We depend on biodiversity for our food. The world's major food plants are grains, vegetables, and fruits, which have been bred from plants in the wild. Wild plants are the source of genes for breeding new varieties of plants. These varieties might be bred to be resistant to disease or to be grown in a warmer **climate** or in poor soil. When these plants become extinct, their useful genes are lost.

Medicine

About 40 percent of all prescription drugs come from chemicals that have been extracted from plants. Scientists discover new, useful plant chemicals every year. The United States National Cancer Institute discovered that 70 percent of plants found to have anticancer properties were rain forest plants. When plant species become extinct, the chemicals within them are lost forever. The lost chemicals may have been important in the making of new medicines.

Did You Know?

Walnuts, apples, and plums all come from trees that originally grew in temperate forests. Humans have **domesticated** wild fruit and nut trees over thousands of years.

Quality of Life

Biodiversity is important to our quality of life. Animals and plants inspire wonder. They are part of our **heritage**. Animals that live in temperate forests, such as squirrels, foxes, wolves, and badgers, have featured in children's stories for hundreds of years. These stories connect people to the natural world.

Many popular children's stories feature animals that live in temperate forests, such as foxes. These stories show how biodiversity can inspire our imagination and improve our quality of life.

Extinct Species

Ten species of moas once lived in New Zealand forests and other habitats. Moas were giant flightless birds. They were preyed on by Haast's eagle, the world's largest eagle. People first arrived in New Zealand around the year 1100, and they hunted the moas to extinction by about 1500. With its prey gone, Haast's eagle also became extinct.

Temperate Forests of the World

Temperate forests are found in the temperate zones of the world. In the south, this is the area between the Tropic of Capricorn and the Antarctic Circle. In the north, this is the area between the Tropic of Cancer and the Arctic Circle.

Types of Temperate Forest

Temperate forests are less dense than rain forests and less open than woodlands. Scientists sometimes define a temperate forest as an area of trees taller than 33 feet (10 meters), with a **canopy** that covers 50 to 80 percent of the sky. There are four main types of temperate forests.

Did You Know?

Rain forests are a type of dense forest, with a canopy that blocks out more than 80 percent of the sky. They can be either temperate or **tropical**.

Temperate forests are mostly found in the Northern Hemisphere, in North America, Europe, and Asia. Some temperate forests are found in southern South America and eastern Australia.

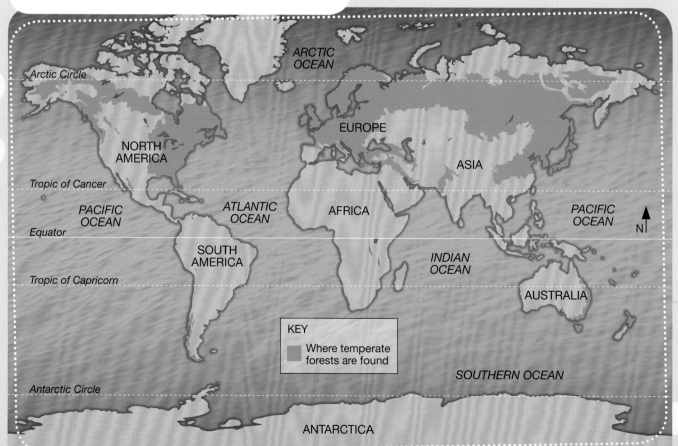

ARCTIC OCEAN

Arctic Circle

EUROPE

NORTH AMERICA

ASIA

Tropic of Cancer

PACIFIC OCEAN

ATLANTIC OCEAN

AFRICA

PACIFIC OCEAN

N

Equator

SOUTH AMERICA

INDIAN OCEAN

Tropic of Capricorn

AUSTRALIA

KEY

Where temperate forests are found

SOUTHERN OCEAN

Antarctic Circle

ANTARCTICA

Deciduous Forest

Deciduous forests have broad-leaved flowering trees, such as oak, elm, plane, and poplar. These trees lose their leaves in the winter. The deciduous forests of New England, in the eastern United States, are famous for their maple trees, which have leaves that turn a spectacular red in the fall.

Evergreen Forest

Evergreen forests have evergreen flowering trees, such as eucalyptus and acacia, which keep their leaves year-round. This type of forest is widespread in southern and eastern Australia. *Eucalyptus regnans*, the world's tallest flowering plant, grows where rainfall is high. Some specimens have grown to more than 300 feet (90 m) tall.

Coniferous Forest

Coniferous forests have conifers, such as redwood, pine, and fir, which are cone-bearing trees. These forests are often found in cold climates, such as in Norway and Finland. The waxy leaves of conifers help them survive freezing temperatures.

Mixed Forest

Mixed forests have a mixture of broadleaf and coniferous trees. The forests of the Adirondacks in New York State have a mixture of deciduous birches and beeches, and coniferous red and white pines.

Deciduous Leaves and Evergreen Leaves

Deciduous trees lose their leaves in the winter. These leaves are thin and would freeze in the cold weather. Before the leaves fall, nutrients flow out of the leaves and are stored in the tree's branches and trunk. Evergreen trees in temperate forests have thick, waxy leaves that protect the leaves from freezing. They stay on the tree all year round.

In this mixed forest in Europe, different species of deciduous and evergreen trees grow side by side.

Temperate Forest Biodiversity

Each type of temperate forest has its own biodiversity. Climate and soil type influence which tree species grow in the forest. In turn, this affects which animal species live there.

Temperate Forest Layers

A temperate forest has several layers of **vegetation**. The uppermost layer is the canopy, which is formed by the leaves and branches of the tallest trees. Beneath this layer is an **understory** of young trees and shrubs. In moist temperate forests, there may be ferns and mosses. The ground layer, known as the forest floor, has grasses and herbs.

Each layer supports different animal species. In a North American mixed temperate forest, different bird species find their food in different forest layers. Winter wrens search for insects close to the ground, while nuthatches hunt for insects on tree trunks. In the canopy, crossbills feed on pine seeds. Red-tailed hawks soar above the canopy, scanning the ground for prey.

canopy

Temperate forests are made up of three main layers of vegetation.

understory

forest floor

Decomposers such as fungi recycle nutrients by breaking down dead plant material in a forest.

Soil Types

The type of soil in a temperate forest is important because it affects the biodiversity of the forest. Soil types may be sandy and well drained, or rich in clay and poorly drained. They may be **fertile** or infertile, shallow or deep. In southern Australian forests, different types of eucalyptus trees are found in different soils. Messmate trees may be the dominant species in well-drained soils, but where the soil becomes heavier, manna gums may dominate. This affects where koalas can be found, because koalas feed on the leaves of manna gums, but not on messmate leaves.

Decomposing Material

Dead material on the forest floor, such as fallen bark and leaf litter, supports a great diversity of organisms called decomposers. Decomposers are fungi and invertebrates that feed on dead material and break it down, or decompose it. This process releases nutrients back into the soil, and these nutrients are used by growing plants. The decomposers themselves are food for forest animals such as birds, lizards, and spiders.

Billions of Beetles

There are more species of beetle than there are species of any other type of animal. Many beetle species are found in leaf litter. A study of a mixed temperate forest in California found 287 species of beetles living in the leaf litter.

Temperate Forest Ecosystems

Living and nonliving things, and the **interactions** between them, make up temperate forest ecosystems. Living things are plants, fungi, and animals. Nonliving things are the soil, the leaf litter, and the climate.

Food Chains and Food Webs

A very important way that different species interact is by eating or consuming other species. This transfers energy and nutrients from one organism to another. A food chain illustrates this flow of energy, by showing what eats what. Food chains are best set out in a diagram. A food web shows how many different food chains fit together.

This North American temperate forest food web is made up of several food chains. In one food chain, acorns from oak trees are eaten by gray squirrels, which in turn are eaten by red-tailed hawks.

Other Interactions

Nonliving and living things in a temperate forest interact in other ways, too. In the forests of North America, fires burn in summer, killing tree seedlings and many animals. After the trees have burned, more light reaches the ground, and grasses grow densely in the ash of the leaf litter. Grazing animals such as deer come to feed on the grass, and as the grass matures, seed-eaters such as mice arrive. In turn, **predators** such as owls and coyotes are attracted to the forest to hunt and feed.

Temperature and day length affect **migratory** birds and **hibernating** bears. When the days get shorter and the air gets cooler in the fall, many birds fly south to warmer places. Black bears dig their dens and begin their long hibernation. In the spring, the bears emerge, ready to feed. The birds return in the spring, too.

Fires are a natural part of many temperate forest ecosystems in the United States and Australia.

Did You Know?

Summer fires in the temperate forests of California and southeastern Australia are the fiercest of any fires in the world. Dry air, fuel, and high temperatures create ideal conditions for fires, which are started by humans or by lightning strikes.

Threats to Temperate Forests

Temperate forests around the world are under threat from activities such as land-clearing and **invasive species**. Many native species lose their habitats and face extinction.

Biodiversity Hotspots

There are about thirty-four regions in the world that have been identified as biodiversity hotspots. These hotspots are regions that have very high biodiversity that is under severe threat from human activities. Biodiversity hotspots have many **endemic species**. The whole of New Zealand is considered a biodiversity hotspot, including its temperate forests.

New Zealand Kauri Forests

New Zealand's temperate kauri forests are located in the far north of its North Island. Kauri trees can live for 2,000 years and grow 130 feet (40 m) tall. Their trunks can be more than 13 feet (4 m) thick.

Many endemic tree species grow in a kauri forest, along with endemic ferns and grasses. The North Island kiwi and kokako are endemic bird species, and the kauri snail is a large, meat-eating endemic species. New Zealand's only two native mammals are found in the kauri forests. Both are bat species.

Tāne Mahuta is the largest kauri tree in the biodiversity hotspot of New Zealand. It is 167 feet (51 m) tall and between 1,250 and 2,500 years old.

The endangered kokako of New Zealand's temperate forests is threatened by invasive mammals such as black rats.

Threats to Kauri Forest Biodiversity

Kauri forests once covered 4,650 square miles (12,000 sq km) of New Zealand. Land-clearing for farming has reduced this area to just 300 square miles (800 sq km).

Today, invasive species are the greatest threat to kauri forest biodiversity. In the 1800s, European settlers introduced thirty-four mammal species into New Zealand. Many of these mammals, including weasels, black rats, dogs, and cats, are predators that prey on native birds and their eggs. Other invasive species, such as deer and brushtail possums, heavily graze many kauri forest plants.

Conserving Kauri Forest Biodiversity

Today, kauri forests are protected from land-clearing. In some areas, cleared land has been replanted with kauri species.

To conserve the forest's biodiversity, invasive species control must continue. New Zealand has a lot of expertise in invasive animal control. Pests such as rats, rabbits, and ermine have been removed from many islands so that endangered native animals can thrive on the islands. Some threatened native species have been relocated to these pest-free islands so that they are safe from invasive species, too.

Agriculture

Temperate forests grow in places that have good soil, plentiful water, and a mild climate. These places are also best suited to agriculture, so it is not surprising that large areas of temperate forest across the world have been cleared for farming.

Effects on Biodiversity

Habitats are destroyed when temperate forests are cleared for agriculture. Some species can become extinct. Red squirrels in Britain cannot survive without forests, because they can only find food and shelter in forest trees.

Clearing forest for farming creates new habitats. Some forest animals can take advantage of these changes. A badger can gather food in open farmland, but it needs enough forest to be able to dig burrows, called setts, for shelter and breeding. Deer, too, will graze in open farmland but use patches of forest for shelter.

Clearing for farmland creates open habitats, which are the preferred habitats of merlins and magpies. These birds increase in number, but warblers and woodpeckers lose their habitats and their population falls.

Europeans began to clear forests in the northeastern United States after the arrival of English settlers aboard the Mayflower in 1620. Three hundred years later, most of the temperate forest had been cleared for farmland.

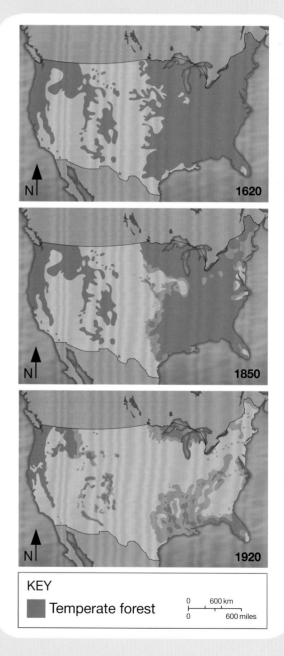

1620

1850

1920

KEY

Temperate forest

0   600 km

0   600 miles

Fragmented Habitats

Trees that are on even ground are often cleared for agriculture, leaving fragments or patches of forest on steep slopes where farming machinery cannot reach. Forest patches are important habitats for many species, but many animals cannot move between patches to breed outside their groups. In time, animals in a group may become inbred and closely related to one another. This loss of genetic diversity makes the group vulnerable to disease, because individuals are very similar and if one is affected by disease, it is likely that all will become affected.

When land is cleared for farming, fragmented forest habitats are created. Each fragment of forest is isolated and many animals are stranded, as if on islands.

To help stop inbreeding, strips of forest can be replanted along creeks and ridges, linking the islands of forest habitat. These strips are called wildlife corridors. They allow animals from different patches to meet and interbreed.

Loss of Knowledge

All over the world, indigenous people have used forest plants for a variety of purposes, from food to medicine to insect repellent. This knowledge has been gathered over many hundreds of years. In the past, a lot of this knowledge was lost when new settlers removed indigenous people from their lands and cleared forests for farming.

Invasive Species

Introduced species are nonnative species that are introduced accidentally or deliberately into a habitat. If they thrive and spread, they become invasive species. Invasive species threaten the biodiversity of temperate forests.

How Are Species Introduced?

Some invasive species are introduced into forests deliberately. The brushtail possum was brought to New Zealand from Australia in 1837 so that settlers would have a source of food and fur. By 1860, it was widespread in New Zealand's forests.

Some species are brought deliberately into a new country, but then escape into other habitats. Runaway pet cats may become **feral** and hunt forest animals. European honeybees can escape from their hives to form wild hives in forests. These insects compete with native insects and birds for nectar. An introduced plant can spread from gardens when its seed is carried by the wind or spread in bird droppings. There may be no diseases that kill the plant species and no animals that eat it. This means it could spread uncontrollably.

The brushtail possum is protected in Australia, but it is a serious pest in New Zealand, where it was introduced.

The Destruction of the American Chestnut

In the past in some forests of the eastern United States, one in four trees was an American chestnut tree. This tree grows to a height of 164 feet (50 m), and its wood was widely used for building. Sometime soon after 1900, the species began to die out. The trees were being killed by chestnut blight fungus, an organism native to Japan and China. The fungus was probably introduced to New York State through infected wood or imported trees. It spread quickly.

By 1940, almost all of an estimated 4 billion American chestnut trees had been killed. Today, blight-resistant trees are being bred from the few specimens that survived. The American Chestnut Foundation is a conservation organization that replants these trees in areas that were once chestnut forests.

Some Invasive Species of Temperate Forests

SPECIES	ORIGIN	WHERE IT WAS INTRODUCED	HOW IT WAS INTRODUCED	BIODIVERSITY THREAT
English ivy	Europe	Southeastern Australia and parts of the United States	As a garden plant	Smothers ground plants
Japanese climbing fern	Japan	Southeastern United States	As a garden plant	Smothers forest plants
Domestic cat	Europe	Many countries	As a pet	Preys on native species
Brushtail possum	Australia	New Zealand	To begin a fur trade	Eats many forest plants

Logging

Temperate forests have been harvested for their lumber for hundreds of years. Today, in many countries, logging continues to be a major threat to the biodiversity of these forests.

Types of Logging

There are different ways of logging a forest. Some forests, or parts of forests, are clear-felled, which means that every tree in the area is cut down. Once the logs are removed, the remaining wood and small plants may be burned to encourage regrowth. Other forests are selectively logged. This means that only the trees that are commercially valuable are cut down.

Short-term Effects of Logging

Whichever way a forest is logged, its biodiversity is affected in many ways. The use of heavy machinery damages the understory and forest soil. It kills animals and destroys their burrows and nests. Roads are built, allowing introduced plants and animals to be carried into the forest by logging trucks. More dirt enters forest streams and they become filled with **silt**.

Logging changes forest habitats completely and has both short-term and long-term effects on biodiversity.

Conservationists try to help Leadbeater's possums by installing nest boxes in forests where trees are too young to have natural hollows.

Long-term Effects of Logging

Logging changes the plant composition of a forest. Natural forests usually contain both young and old trees, but when an area is clear-felled, the trees that regrow are of the same age. This is unsuitable habitat for some animal species and this can have long-term effects. Leadbeater's possum is a small, endangered marsupial of southeastern Australia that needs forest habitats that have many young trees, a few old trees, and a dense understory of acacia trees. The possum feeds on insects and sap from young trees, and it shelters and breeds in nest hollows in old trees. The acacias provide it with safe crossing points between trees. These possums are losing their habitats because replanted forests do not have a mix of trees.

Carolina Parakeet

On February 21, 1918, the last known specimen of the Carolina parakeet died at Cincinnati Zoo in Ohio. The Carolina parakeet was the only parrot species native to the eastern United States. The logging of its forest habitat was the main cause of its extinction.

Climate Change

The world's average temperature is rising because levels of certain gases, such as carbon dioxide, are increasing in Earth's atmosphere. The temperature increase is causing other climate changes. These changes affect temperate forest habitats.

Effects of Climate Change on Forests

Scientists are uncertain exactly how temperate forests will be affected by climate change. They do know that the amount of rainfall and where it falls will change. Scientists predict that in general the United States will become warmer and wetter over the next fifty years. This should increase the area of temperate forest. In the southeast and southwest of the United States, however, rainfall is predicted to decrease. This would lead to an increase in the number and intensity of fires, causing forests to be replaced by woodlands, shrublands, and grasslands.

Invasive Species

Climate change will affect the distribution of introduced plants and animals in forests. In Australia, an increase in temperature will probably allow the introduced plant lantana to spread southward into wet forests. With reduced rainfall, an introduced plant pest called gorse is likely to retreat south. This is because gorse cannot tolerate very dry conditions.

Temperate forests in the United States might increase in size as the climate becomes warmer and wetter.

Bark beetles bore into trees and lay their eggs, then their young feed on the bark and wood, which can kill the trees. Climate change is causing beetle populations to grow.

Bark Beetles

Since 1990, bark beetles have killed millions of trees in temperate forests along the western coast of North America. Bark beetle species are native to these forests, but their effects have never been so severe. Scientists believe that a rise in average temperatures has meant that beetles survive longer and reproduce more, and reduced rainfall has weakened the trees' resistance to beetle attack.

Disease

Red band needle blight is a fungal disease that has recently become a serious threat to lodgepole pines in British Columbia, in Canada. The spread of this disease is due to an increase in summer rainfall, which allows the fungus to thrive.

Did You Know?

Earth's climate has changed many times over millions of years. About 10,000 years ago, during the last ice age, most of Canada and northern Europe were covered in icesheets that were nearly 2 miles (3 kilometers) thick.

Temperate Forest Conservation

Conservation is the protection, preservation, and wise use of resources. Temperate forests are a valuable resource and their biodiversity needs to be conserved. Research, education, laws, and breeding programs all play a part in forest conservation.

Research

Research projects are carried out to find out information about temperate forest ecosystems. This information shows us why forest ecosystems are important, and it helps people make decisions about how to protect forests and their biodiversity. Scientific studies have shown that temperate forests store more carbon in every 2.5 acres (0.01 sq km) than rain forests do. When these forests are cleared and burned, the carbon is released into the atmosphere as carbon dioxide, adding to climate change. Conserving temperate forests means that carbon remains stored and is not released.

The Importance of Temperate Forests

Temperate forests are very important for many reasons. They:

- are habitat for many animal species
- are great places to visit
- absorb carbon dioxide and release oxygen
- filter pollutants from water and bind the soil, preventing **erosion**.

Amount of Carbon Stored By Different Types of Forest

TYPE OF FOREST	AVERAGE AMOUNT OF CARBON STORED PER ACRE (TONS)
Temperate *Eucalyptus regnans* forests of southeastern Australia	1,269
Temperate forests in high-rainfall areas	168
Subtropical forests	131
Temperate forests in low-rainfall areas	79
Tropical rain forests	76

Education

Educating people about temperate forests is essential for forest conservation. Information from scientists must be passed on to people, such as students, loggers, and tourists. When people are shown how temperate forests are important to their own lives, they are more likely to help conserve them.

Protected Areas and Breeding Programs

Temperate forest habitat may be protected by national parks and reserves, and this helps to conserve forest wildlife too. Breeding programs in zoos can save temperate forest species from extinction. These programs are necessary when a species's numbers are very low or when its habitat is endangered. Animals bred in zoos may be released back into the wild if areas of suitable habitat exist.

The highly endangered Iberian lynx lives in Mediterranean forest in Spain. These animals are being bred in captivity, and scientists plan to reintroduce them into the wild to increase the small population.

Laws to Protect Forest Species

In Tasmania, in Australia, the government passed a law that all pet cats must be desexed, so that they cannot breed, and microchipped, so that they can be identified electronically. This is to stop feral cat numbers from growing. There are more than 150,000 feral cats in Tasmania, and these cats prey on native forest species.

The Bialowieza Forest covers 580 square miles (1,500 sq km) of Poland and Belarus. Unlike other European forests, it has been mostly undisturbed by humans. Because of this, it has many species that are found nowhere else in Europe.

Bialowieza Forest Biodiversity

The Bialowieza Forest is the last wild **habitat** of Europe's largest mammal, the wisent, also called the European bison. Other rare mammals of the forest are the European lynx, European badger, gray wolf, elk, otter, and masked shrew.

The main evergreen tree species in the Bialowieza Forest are conifers, such as Scots pine and Norway spruce. The main deciduous species are aspen, white birch, hornbeam, English oak, alder, linden, lime, goat willow, Norway maple, and ash.

Numbers of Known Species in the Bialowieza Forest

TYPE OF ORGANISM	KNOWN SPECIES
Animals	At least 12,000
Insects	More than 8,500
Birds	232
Mammals	62
Amphibians	12
Reptiles	7
Plants	At least 1,400
Liverworts (type of small, flowerless plant)	800
Vascular plants (plants that have veins that carry water and nutrients through the stems and leaves)	632
Fungi	More than 3,000
Lichen	254

Ancient Home of Wisents

The Bialowieza Forest is the last remaining part of the deciduous and mixed temperate forest that once covered much of Europe. It is about 10,000 years old. Other forests in Europe have been cleared but the Bialowieza Forest has been protected, in different ways, for the past 600 years. This protection began in the 1400s when King Władysław Jagiełło banned hunting and tree-cutting in the forest, so that he would have wisents to hunt. The kings and czars who followed him also protected the wisent and its habitat.

During World War I (1914–1918), German troops occupied the forest. They shot forest animals such as wisents for food. By 1919, the wisent was extinct in the wild.

In the 1920s, a breeding program was begun to save the species, using fifty-four wisents from zoos and private collections. In 1929, 20.5 square miles (53 sq km) of the forest were made a national park and a few wisents were released. Today, more than 540 wisents live in the forest.

Wisent numbers in the Bialowieza Forest are recovering as a result of a breeding program.

CASE STUDY: The Bialowieza Forest

World Heritage Site

The heritage importance of Bialowieza Forest biodiversity is recognized by the United Nations. In 1971, an area of 19 square miles (48 sq km) at the center of the Bialowieza Forest National Park was named as a **World Heritage Site**. In 1992, another 17.3 square miles (45 sq km) were added. In 1996, the total area of national parks in Poland was increased to 40.5 square miles (105 sq km).

Protecting the Forest

Despite its World Heritage listing, only about 10 percent of the Bialowieza Forest is fully protected from logging and hunting. The national parks in Poland and Belarus cover just 58.7 square miles (152 sq km) of forest. Within the park boundaries, there are areas where no vehicles are permitted. These areas have been set aside for special protection, because vehicles compact the soil, disturb wildlife, and carry in weed seeds on their tires. Today, logging and hunting continue in the forest outside the national parks.

Some parts of the Bialowieza Forest that are not protected have been cleared by farmers for crops. Conservation organizations such as the World Wildlife Fund (WWF) are campaigning to achieve full protection for the entire forest.

The Bialowieza Forest is the only remaining example of natural mixed forest in Europe, so the protection offered by the Bialowieza Development Program is very important.

Bialowieza Development Program

In 2009, a conference about the conservation of the Bialowieza Forest took place in the national park. Scientists, local people, the United Nations, conservation organizations, and the Polish and Belarusian governments attended the conference. The Bialowieza Development Program (BDP) was announced and official agreements were signed. The BDP aims to triple the area of protected forest, and also develop industries that provide work for local people but which do not damage the forest or its biodiversity.

The Importance of the Bialowieza Forest

Professor Alan Weisman, a science writer, spoke about the Bialowieza Forest at the BDP conference. He said that, as one of the oldest intact forests, the Bialowieza Forest:

"provides a baseline of what healthy temperate forests might have been like. A baseline is an invaluable tool, because from one we can track changes, especially changes caused by human activity, far more easily than we can in a forest that has been severely altered by humans."

What Is the Future of Temperate Forests?

Temperate forests are under severe threat from human activities. It may seem impossible to stop their destruction, but when threats are removed, biodiversity decline can be slowed or stopped. Some species may reappear and increase biodiversity.

What Can You Do for Temperate Forests?

You can help protect forests in several ways.

- Find out about temperate forests. Why are they important and what threatens them?
- If you live in or near a forest, you can join volunteer groups who replant cleared land with forest species.
- Become a responsible consumer. Do not litter and do not buy products that have been harvested from forests.
- If you are concerned about forests in your area, or beyond, write to or e-mail your local newspaper, your state congressperson, or a local representative. Know what you want to say, set out your arguments, be sure of your facts, and ask for a reply.

Useful Websites

- **http://wwf.panda.org/about_our_earth/ecoregions/about/habitat_types/habitats/temperate_forests**
  This WWF website contains information about temperate forest habitats, ecosystems and wildlife.

- **www.biodiversityhotspots.org**
  This website has information about the richest and most threatened areas of biodiversity on Earth.

- **www.iucnredlist.org**
  The International Union for the Conservation of Nature (IUCN) Red List has information about threatened plant and animal species.

Glossary

adapt   Change in order to survive.

canopy   Leaves of the upper layer of plants in a forest or woodland.

carbon dioxide   A colorless and odorless gas produced by plants and animals.

climate   The weather conditions in a certain region over a long period of time.

domesticate   To tame and keep or cultivate for the benefit of humans.

ecosystem   The living and nonliving things in a certain area and the interactions between them.

endemic species   Species found only in a particular area.

erosion   Wearing away of soil and rock by wind or water.

extinct   Having no living members.

feral   Wild, especially domestic animals that have gone wild.

fertile   Capable of producing lots of vegetation, possibly due to a high nutrient content.

gene   Segment of deoxyribonucleic acid (DNA) in the cells of a living thing, which determines its characteristics.

habitat   Place where animals, plants, or other living things live.

heritage   Things we inherit and pass on to future generations.

hibernate   Spend the winter in a dormant state (as if in a deep sleep) to conserve energy.

interaction   Action that is taken together or actions that affect each other.

invasive species   Nonnative species that negatively affect their new habitats.

migratory   Moves from one place to another, especially seasonally.

nutrient   Substance that is used by living things for growth.

organism   Animal, plant, or other living thing.

predator   Animal that kills and eats other animals.

silt   Soil and sediments carried in water.

species   A group of animals, plants, or other living things that share the same characteristics and can breed with one another.

tropical   In the hot and humid region between the Tropic of Cancer and the Tropic of Capricorn.

understory   Layer of plants that grows below the canopy of a forest.

vegetation   Plants.

World Heritage Site   A site that is recognized as having great international importance and that is protected by the United Nations Educational, Scientific and Cultural Organization (UNESCO).

Index